The
Backwaters
Press

THE BACKWATERS PRIZE IN POETRY

Dear Wallace

JULIE CHOFFEL

THE BACKWATERS PRESS

An imprint of the University of Nebraska Press

Acknowledgments for the use of copyrighted
material appear on pages 79–80, which constitute
an extension of the copyright page.

⊚

Library of Congress Cataloging-in-Publication Data
Names: Choffel, Julie, author.
Title: Dear wallace / Julie Choffel.
Description: [Lincoln]: The Backwaters Press,
an imprint of the University of Nebraska Press,
2024. | Series: The Backwaters Prize in Poetry
Identifiers: LCCN 2024016821
ISBN 9781496240064 (paperback)
ISBN 9781496241191 (epub)
ISBN 9781496241207 (pdf)
Subjects: BISAC: POETRY / American /
General | LCGFT: Poetry.
Classification: LCC PS3603.H636 D43 2024 |
DDC 811/.6—dc23/eng/20240415
LC record available at https://lccn.loc.gov/2024016821

For Jason, Cora, Omi, and Leo

One might say that my father lived alone.

—Holly Stevens

CONTENTS

Dear Wallace

Dear Wallace,

Where did you hide the blood? I've gone into the woods and partied with the critters, told the children to wait in the cave. But nothing came to me. I hid all the history, saving up just to write this instead of sleeping. Could you cleanse me in the work of your sisters, they who move us through the everyday?

By now it's beyond nice out. All the light hoarded for a brief and blinding season. The dead voles shaken by exposure, *it looks a lot like engine oil and tastes like being poor and small*. We loop from interior to perimeter so many times! I almost died in the dark, but my own life caught like a bone in the throat of another.

I saw the forest open and close around the scent trail. And I went for the children.

*

Your sentiment like a boulder
careening down a marked path;
I step aside.
Your logic so *sure*.
I could practically punch you in the gut
but instead I listen
to the little toad
in your voice.

Did you ever have to search
for an old way again?

*

They say mother is the boredom

                   of invention.

Stripes, stripes, stripes, spots.
How was it
in the business of risk
did you talk
     about markets
         while your mind
scoffed?

     There was a little anarchy today.
It was all about sound.

Dear Wallace,

What was it like, then?
All that money
       in all this wind.
Did you have friends
       who loved
what you loved
or did you also
       forget to call?

It's a cold, cold mess now
you know.

       What did you
hate?

*

Nearly everyone will play along with a man.

The future pummels us. That's why we look back. The kids want a dog, my husband wants sex. It's a picture book really. I just want a setting. Before, *we* weren't even here. And I already missed them then like I miss myself now. *Mama, you know what's coming up?* I usually do. These poems aren't going to write themselves.

Pretend with me.

Dear Wallace,

I guess you never had to listen
to a highway?
It's everywhere now
whispering
this used to bother me
but now I think
it's a reminder
of bloodlines,
kinship & elsewheres.

Mostly it takes me
shopping, another
task you loved
a little too?
      Here's fruit, vegetable, bread.
      Fate in a dish, pending.
Sometimes when I think there's nothing and no
one left, I imagine the folds of my brain
      holding something hostage.
Negotiations useless.
I wait it out.

What did you sacrifice?

      What do you look into
for others?

*

So I've also wondered
    if you knew anything like
the ridicule of suburbia.
        All the little babies' fists
raised in the autumn air.

You say geranium like a household word
but still it's
European? A vagary.
    School me
on the ways of a different era
when one could ride
        an entire wave
    of another's making.

We're all as genuine as we seem.

Appearances like trash and art
        passing hand to hand.

*

The narrow stream runs short, sweet
through the nunnery's greenway and once
it fed an orchard, or so I saw on the old maps
and I'm ever since looking for signs of those days
and haven't found a thing.

These days, the nuns are all passing
away and I wonder if the ground feels them go
each one who used to walk there
in some sort of god's love. The oldest
may have known the fruit; another may have cried
into the stream when the spirit declined her calls.

When I look at their graveyard, the same story
happens again and again like an overshared link
in my own time telling us the oldest words
in our language. *Worm* was one.
Long as a syllable could ride on a stoic tongue.

*

If things change not for some time
and then all at once

which part is this?

They say invention is the boredom
of mothers.

We have a dozen flavors of tea.
We have no time to waste.
We have meeting after meeting.

Welcome to the clan of
name-the-next-beast.

Enter the floodlands
where, mostly, nothing happens.

Watch us waiting,
watch us practice the rescue
until it becomes a near-death performance.

Dear Wallace,

We may share this same gray noon
December creeps up and away in
recklessly toying
with the eyes

some guys have all the luck
mine's okay

to survive, I pull farther and farther out
from the thing

but you
you dive and dive and I
marvel at the trajectories of cockle shells in your clouds
the gas giants dispersing while
tick tock, we all arrive.

*

My whole brain is here for it,
chanting the secular rosary,
the old flame in my hand.

What am I learning anymore
but doubt.

Tell me how to be ready
I want to be the one to walk in the sun
when I'm the same lesson over and over.

Is it opportunistic
to assume our suffering
has anything in common
when grief is never the same thing twice?

All the grandpas
we hardly even know
shouting from the other room.

My idea of fun—
to run in the field,
tripping over the new names
of each soft thing.

*

Today everyone managed
to put on their pants. It doesn't
matter how much I teach them
if all they want to know is
the words of the void.

Today the sun rose and the void
was undetectable. If anything,
it runneth over
my heart
my many hearts
my abundance of aspects
one with a great levity
one with a cracked-ice pond
one with a handwritten note
one with a feather boa
one with a snake tongue
one with a thorny crown
and one to grow on, to keep
talking me into
or out of it.

*

Sometimes I'm rabid as you.
I mean, I'm in my bathrobe.
I'm hoarse and
haven't even said anything yet.

But I foam and froth
at the edges.
I think of things.
But I keep them with me.

*

Who carves the way for mothers?

I have no land
or future to my name,
no way with clothes
or forecasts.
A few laughs.

That old sublime, sun on floorboards.
What was it about your home?

Kindling? Pantry moths? Tarot?

Dear Wallace,

Was it lovely
to live in your head
fireside & bedecked in
materials
for the next front

the domain of law
like a fucking of the word
every night
after dinner

& did you love
only the ones
who bent to your
meaning
or were you
not mad

just organized?

*

But this is a swamp, they said.

               We're over it
futile   slick pond
of dumb potential, murk, trash

loved only   for a density   of living cells,
we mean water   quicksand   or

slogging,
our horse has been   drowning
              for hours,
                    cypress, orchid,
bones lost
           in the skeins.

We mean battle is lonesome
                 or blood comes fast.

   The monsters
of maximum return   will get you every turn,

         time lapse
         or voodoo, Reubens or Rubens
                   the entire body
the entire time.

*

Many, many animals and insects
lay eggs and then die
or give birth and die
or raise their young
and die when the time is come.

Humans keep living, may outlive even
their own kids' lives but still
there's a beginning of the end of the self
in that making.

And clearly
the kids make us older
accelerate our
realization & our
dying so what
is left of
invention, mother
of boredom.

These faint touches of light
are almost enough.

Four o'clock is everything.

When I see my want on the horizon
I know what it's trying to tell me.

Dear Wallace,

I wish you had written a
desperate poem.

Were you never?

A regular, boring life.

A regular imagination.

A running list
of palpable notions.

Dear Wallace,

O what you managed!

> Our complicity
> just cities marked by money—
> bodies in and out of health.

Every claim to care
for the flesh we live in & the land
we're on, we submit our forms.
A hundred years ago
your body was your own,
your market potential
endless.

> The way we love
> the other through that. To live
> alongside you as the shared
> burden I am. Our way out's
> in getting in.

A tide is what comes and goes,
now you see it, now you don't.

> I try to break our patterns
> in small gestures that take lifetimes
> to accrue. I take you up and up
> the mountain only to slay another lamb.

Or, how do we put a price on what we love.
Like you, wondering what Sunday is for.
You, in a place made for you.
Not like you at all, a mother
makes a place for others.
Like all of us, if we're lucky.

*

Shall we go back and unname it?
The origin for a kind of mind.
We all deserve a self untold.

The inklings in my house
scattering, they say, *I found your idea
and I put it in my pocket.*

We all have a diary
of generous entry.

*Now I'm the mom   and he's the cat.
Now let's switch.*

The economy leaking its jobs   and
calling it a blessing
modernity sounding like   maternity
to hide its ruin.

*Now here is a tower
with nothing to do in it.*

In a parallel universe
the poet is the survivor.

Let's hold hands 'til we're dead.

*

Across the street
       they are digging graves
with a tiny excavator
           in the off-light
of winter
         and I'm thinking of you
in your off-light abilities
            the men are quiet
respectful of their task
              and exacting
with long handled shovels to
               finish the work
and a ladder
                for climbing out
and this is what I do
                  I listen
I lay it down
                 hush
let us
            acknowledge
the holes, emerging
            in time,
even the crawler   nearly
           sleeping
on its loop.

Dear Wallace,

Though we inhabit the same place
it's many places now
it's a hundred places

and when you lived, it looked like you
in every face   ready for painting

then it moved on

so it doesn't look like me now
thankfully it doesn't look like any one
painter & it doesn't need our eye

but it does need
something ancient, something unused
perhaps your dough & someone else's
attention span

what does it mean to contribute
to art & is it anything more than living

the dictionary
tries to pronounce us

men today saying they can't be
themselves anymore

I'm not your wife
but I hope she challenged you
like a universe
in a dress.

*

It's true that sometimes the sun

reflects brightly off the snow
and citizens ski in city parks
like they just believe in things

we are for real, you and I,
about all the sound
already and not yet made

though my frequency is lower:

when the fox ran down my street
and through the yard
it was all that mattered
to the fox

we could swap theories
I could make the noise
and you could listen.

*

Waiting in your neighborhood
at the JCC
what can I say
I like the exposure of the parking lot
and the riptide of exercise just within reach.

Some state of affairs
the world wide with grief
crying in its cars
wishing to be taken out
of its mind, wishing pictures
could fix it, all us
aestheticians in the plague.

Every door
keeps trying
the outside again.
Our hands wringing
in our ears
a higher calling
just out of reach

and through the thought of it
the act returns,
our dreams sheltered,
then on the run.

*

An imposition:
If you didn't deal in reality then,

I suppose you could now.
My kids want to bend your ear.

The listening tunnel,
claustrophobic,
tunes only to love and fear.

If you take my children away from me
what makes me a mother
and if I title my poems *Dear No One*,
what makes me a peer
and how do I find what is seldom heard

out on the range?
Dear kids, my kids, tenderhearted beasts, fortune-worthy saviors, sceptics,
write back sincerely to me.

*

Fortunately, my kid was wrong
when she said *the squirrel is up in the tree, eating a raven*.
I take her very seriously
as she is careful
and it was like a sign
of the end times.

Of course, I don't believe in end times.
But I am pretty sure that I'm baking a ruined bread
that's not rising
as I write this—a poor
fungus in the envelope.

It is a treat to be taken seriously.

Beloveds so often
dismiss one another.

Boredom invents sex, then mothers.

Yes, I meant a hawk.

*

Sanctuary.

It's what they taught us to teach the kids
when we taught poems. *What's yours?*
we'd say.

Maybe it's not a house.
Just not thinking in sentences.

The moon's side-eye
        looping over my mess
            my mess
maybe I'm starting to like it.

*

But mothers like yours
inverted boredom: Oh! Oh! Oh!

(Sometimes the miniature dino
is discovered in the enormous fort
inscribed in the handmade book.)

Sometimes we invite the rude over for a drink.

(Sarcastic as fuck.)
(Fine.)

Invention, we're taught, works backward
anyway: first *fusion*, then its *uses*.

I do it for the joy it brings
because I'm a joyful girl.
Who was more important
or had the most fun
or ground up the world and spit it out again more?

(Make it new or make it blue
and black and rainbow camo
and stuff it in a seed packet that you
scatter on another sick day:
It's the little things!)

Of course it was a father who said
too many choices make a sad boy.
I teach a class on the rhetoric of money
and put it in my pocket.

(I could have gone into so many fields.)

My mother's laugh
distills an entire memory,
a better word
than your entire cadre.
I watch your ideas go to sleep.
Look how they breathe, perfect and pink
with the blush of the day behind them.
You wish they could stay like that forever
but alas, as they say
observation effect and all that.

(Yes, honey, I'm right here. Yes I see
the hot lava.)

Dear Wallace,

The difference is you were writing from your home.

The difference is the greater metropolitan area.

The difference is a retained aesthetic.

The difference is the color of our bruises.

The difference is the war.

The difference is who is still listening.

The difference is I was trying to tell you.

The difference is I'm already holding so many inventions.

The difference is literal.

The difference is your secretary.

The difference is a room.

The difference is the everlasting musk of vernix.

The difference is the shape of my mouth saying *ah*.

The difference is me time.

The difference is in my centermost thought.

The difference is your feigned objectivity.

The difference is a wilderness rendered in plastic.

The difference is the rupture of every continuum.

The difference is held fast by a safety pin.

The difference is my risk.

The difference is parenting culture.

The difference is less than one degree of latitude.

Plants and animals, the magnetic field, a handful of errant stones.

*

We're all advancing the cause of something.

Well anyway we see the light
and we call it fair or unfair
and we work or we don't
on purpose or accident.
We watch ourselves tick along
the spectrum

of wonder. We love it.
What is the source? The end?
What if no matter is lost between them?
But I disagree
time can be lost
and we lose people like sand,
et cetera,

what was your weakness
and mine.

The self an imploding star,
only faster, why it feels good.
Do we feel so good
now? For a hot minute?

The heat makes me weak
in the knees, makes someone else dead.
There's no calculus
for pleasure.

You never needed a safety net
but could you catch the others
falling all around you?
Did you offer your hands?

*

I'm sure you lost sleep over something
in a poem
or the poem its own form of rest

actually no
it's mostly waking up
and changing my mind.

Dear Wallace,

To espouse, to embrace, to trace
going back to you
        reading the wild
my program responds
        to make you up again

we were some kind of genus
in different forests
        fine, if not fair
I want to see
        what everyone can make

I don't want to explain it
to you
        I want you to explain it to me
the implications
        of your industry

the flowering of your mind
aghast at itself
        & the wife in your life
working as if
        she meant it.

*

I can't stop. But I really

want to know what

you worked against.

Was it me?

It's April, the snowflakes

fatten and slow.

I can't stop.

One day I'll know you

truly. I spread out

the poppy seeds timely

this year, enough

to collect some frost

before the sprint. I

watch a video that tells me

how to live here.

We might as well

try one way as try another

if we can't stop. Rolling

in your grave, your code

cracks and thaws.

An occasion arises;

we bolt.

It's not like you had real

enemies.

*

They hated me today
for my power
a seasonal accident
        no way to predict
        though you could sense it like
quake or storm coming

what if genius is just fucking around really well
lightning strikes, maybe once
maybe twice

I just want to hold them
like when they are sick and simple
but that seems awful
shouldn't I love them most
when they are most free

how do I
not determine their future
nor shrug it off, like it's
        but a dream
verily verily verily verily

I'm the stream
        and the child was enough.

*

I'm making off with
        you
this reverie
        of the mother and the meta
in tandem in no man's hand
        did you think you had
different
        work to do
the table for one now
        laid to waste
how gently we notice
        ourselves
living among others
        connected then
off again
        our
love for the mind
        and time to see it
we answer with joy
        life's a disappointment
and then you live
        to see the guns
melted down
        to alloy
how is there so much iron
        in us
we're asking
        are we dirt or
better than dirt
        the poets I love
are overwhelmed
        bursting at the edges

of the thinkable
        a way out or
back in
        and the rose garden's
a trapdoor
        unbelievable work
for public pleasure
        frugal steps at first
then you realize
        you've saved it all
for nothing
        but your own self
some call this
        woke like
we're suddenly here now
        hiding
under the rainbow
        the premise grasped
and we want to
        change it
and yes
        perception is a wretched
twisted thing
        and yes
the work of many
        makes bloom for few
and you abide, my friend
        you rot with the flowers
but no, the burst of color is not
        the only thing
the awakening is not
        the only awakening

there are days the words
     are nothing
and my dumb heart is it
     an animal
pleasure as when
     clumsy I drop
a fragile thing
     and catch it in the finest
degree of time
     the best part
of every day
     not being awake
but waking
     in the unmade world
to see what we can do
     it feels backward
the slippery poem then
     as when
the errand continues
     so long
I can't remember
     what we were looking for
and it becomes an entirely
     otherwise way.

*

The screen pixelates the yard
a million squares in green
some girls, some girls are only about
that thing
      some girls love the delicate ephemerals
others love the sea
some girls love the WNBA
      but only one loves me
in each tiny frame
a blur

shadow, light, shadow, light
our younger years all about detail
but in age we benefit
from a wider lens

my life is what's
between me and my subject

of all the colors in the world
envy gets the one
that means alive

a plant without green
steals from its host

take what you need
—does the world want to be made?
in no new mass

our house is home to more birds than people
a reassurance of wrens
if there was ever a view for a woman
it was determined by her own eye.

Dear Wallace,

You could say I've been on edge
except that I'm living in the canyon now
instead of peering over

the flying snakes go right by me
eating nothing for days
maybe I'm just scenery now

how lovely
of you to think of me
like a daughter

like a daughter I pitch the tent
at each new site
and scour the place for scorpions

but the craziest part is the music
how it travels the painted walls to me
just to say things
made for my ears by
the long gone   traveling ever since

the craziest part is that I'm in the middle of several lives
and all of them medium rare

and all the flaming hoops hissing
now you see it   now
you forget
that I keep us alive
with the brink as my witness.

*

In the play
are you red-faced
or blue?

*

People don't want to talk about privilege
because we've all had a hard time
    (if mostly okay)
maybe that one time destroyed you

but also partly because
we are assholes
hoarding all the pretense

I am just like, if having a baby or three
was rough for me
               then what the hell for the
totally unsupported   plus there's
a thousand things we don't know about each other

    (hold the phone)

tell me all the ways you were lucky
tell me all the ways you weren't.

*

You're prolific.
You put even my own words in
your mouth.
I'm pro tem, like *no more*
boys in my womb.

The baby boy came out,
followed by another.
The crowd oohed and aahed.

The girl, having arrived
prepared, resisted interpretation.
Said, *I wish I were famous*,
meanwhile, the lamb bleating
like a steak.

I collect only stories
I can use.

*

In the story of the stonecutter
we get so many chances to learn.

Then in stories with mothers, we get horrible—

What's the one thing you would have done differently?

Be less sad? Not
regret? Pay more or
less attention
to the children?

My husband says I suffer
from imposter syndrome. I guess
it's the opposite of delusions of grandeur.

If I could do one thing differently
I'd switch every instance
of *legitimate* and *ephemeral*
with its other.

*

Everyone hates my poems the most

looking jealous or crazy
I go all the way
but everyone's a bad poet
sometimes. Darlin',
this town is real crazy in summer.

Hon, did you have all these barbeques?
People ask you to read nonsense
while audiences browsed?
And the roses—

fuck, I cannot.

     I need a field
     of dull, brassy grasses

the dishes are waiting for me the flies are really happy

and people tell me I'm so great
to be nice

     yawn

you're like this other place.

*

It's like "outdoor living"
before the window units go in
I paid for this
someone paid for this
it wasn't you   it was your shadow

my mom asks if I will miss it when I'm gone
I dunno
but I will not miss your shadow
or all the shadows here

I'm haunting you
with my lack of taste
poets are a lot like stalkers
trailing the details into the dark
and watching them change their clothes

maybe I'm just a troll
hurtling rocks
from the other side

if it wasn't for the screen
the vine would grow right in
and make itself at home.

Dear Wallace,

I probably should have written to Williams. The longer line, the green
world, the love, it's all there, and I want to know what you talked about,
did you ever talk, did his face like a Fiennes brother make you softer and
did you ask him anything, did he look at you like a friend, did he tell you
I would be waiting here for you, did he know it all like his poems. Which
of you the naïf. People always think I'm younger than I am, whatever that
means. I always wanted to be older. Your birthdays, four years apart, your
death days, eight. You the cold open, he the warm body. It's not you, it's
me. Oh brother. Look at us, so American! I'm not, as much; maybe no
one is now. Does this poem make me look old?

*

Why is your archive so dull?
This is the last question I asked myself
before dumping it into the river.
My own last entry reads *1991* or *any year.*
Code for kook. Bathwater, baby.

Young and starry self
much better at listening. Now,
when the sky keens, I talk back.
But it's just me, my mouth against a wall.

And the spirit churning
sends goodwill; O last century, O final
countdown to the ends of kindnesses
let empathy be born
of consuming a sliver of another's fate

implications pointing all
to the playground.
I worked so hard and
all I got was this stupid line.

A temporary thing
came to leave me more real
than I was before.

When were you small
and unimportant
in a place
no one cared for—
we who love to be invited
have to find another way.

My casual creation
calls me out.

Look at your pleasure!
Like you never had a visitor
telling you what to call it.
Like you said no
to everything else.

*

Oh, hello. It's May 1, I'm wearing a coat,

the greens are slowly greening
and the music is old
and no one is trying to kill me.
I'm so grateful
for the ends of things

like anxious starts.

Nostalgia calls, easy
as quicksand. I say no
thank you. You made me
to look for more.

May 2 is nearly here.

My sisters are texting
bits and pieces of songs
so are you
listening to the country
I was not born
to run

just to feel free and be someone.

Read or don't read the comments
Miss Emmylou thought of her own song
but she didn't even write it
okay well
nobody gonna make me do things their way

the lawmen give no fucks
about women singing
about time.

It's a collective loss
if you're paying attention, Wallace,
it's a collective toss-up
what can we catch
in a single grab
I get my lovin' on the run

and all my lullabies are classics.

*

What if the auspices
of influence are merely
offices, interiors in a shadow
carved out from the rest of our time?
What if the holding is as good as the having.
If illusion made off with you
and never brought you home
would you be an award-winning father
would you be the calico fawn in dusk light
or the mother, hunched over
and hunting in the dark?

Dear Wallace,

The closeness is weather, street names, a few remaining animals.

The closeness is boring.

The closeness is our propensity for violence.

The closeness is a duty to see more.

The closeness is whether anyone cares.

The closeness is try me.

The closeness is backup plans.

The closeness is a window and a decent pair of eyes.

The closeness is a flexible concept of time.

The closeness is looking both ways.

The closeness is only figurative.

The closeness is who's in charge.

The closeness is so white.

The closeness is it means very little except when it means very much.

The closeness is less than one degree of latitude.

The closeness is the oak and hickory.

The closeness is the rate of carbon decay.

The closeness is mud.

The closeness is what hasn't happened yet.

*

What if my urgency is the same
as everyone else's
even yours
especially yours
worth the same time
you'd give to hunger.

Did you see it? asked the stranger, standing
on her lawn, looking past me as I ran down her street.
It usually doesn't get that pretty.
A crease of orange in a corner
of the sky. The turning things
we forget to be inside of.

So much of what we do is just
saying hello to the minutes.

Dear Wallace,

The long tidal river
is nothing special.
The broken buildings
are not special.
Your walk home
not special,
your house
not, nor the maple
still growing
in your yard
the afternoon
I stopped by
in the drag of
my very own friction
to touch some
place that pushed me
away.

*

The kids are downstairs with their dad
dancing to Lady Gaga
did I mention what a greatness he is

Go write, he says
I roll my eyes
one minute feels like a decade
another a quark
I contract or expand within it

the landscape's shape is determined
by the cleave of its rocks as they fall

a crystal geology saying how soft
or hard it will bend or break
easy or slow to erode

history is a can of worms
in a world strewn with cans and worms
Mama, help me draw some furniture messed up by cats
It needs to be just right

we all marvel at the final product
I'm the only one laughing at the supply chain
a beast exposed
to culture.

*

The house smells like age (ew)
sounds like apology
(for yelling & poetry)

but we're all agog at the coral reef

"meal prep" under my living
even the fairies need food?
and even with free range
still buying pull-ups

I'm so covered in skin
I'm so *someday you will ache like I ache*
but like good now

okay because new interior
I'm saving up for

the future
is either all about me
or all about everyone else

I feel guilty every time I use a Ziploc
like every stupid time.

*

Hallmark is hiring.
That's a poet's joke.
Really the bored mothers of inventory
are stocking their shelves
with thank-yous; the excited ones
shop for sugar and drugs. I keep
everyone alive and boss around the sun
but even your sun depends upon
you seeing it. Inventors
get bored with mothers but never with
the children, which is where they store
their ideas. Meanwhile the kids are like
too busy. They have other houses to build.
One permit after another. I punch my card
for to the lovers go the spoils.

Dear Wallace,

Now your mosaic trips me up. It's too much,
I can only read a page at a time.
Who else said something beautiful

and slow. The duration
for a stone. So many times I could have written
this poem, but I went to the store instead,
wallowed in distance, researched childcare.
I'm a regular materfamilias

so so lucky
but I can't wash my hands of anything.
Life piling up and up
above me. I know how to sleep
and how to remember.

So I get the dream-along.
In your own way you were trying to save
us. From the heat waves, the warehouses,
the carpel tunnel, the prism of a single self
repeating in the retina.

*

What are ethics of writing about the dead? I've lost—nearly no one.
Having loved living, and still do, I say this, diving into

any given moment. I think of real dying, bodies like horses; a large life laid
down. It is a comfort, prudent and sure. Not much is sure. Not much.

*

Like you I'm blind to the source
of my intent. Are you the scrim?
It feels a little rich
maybe not a bad thing
but it's good to notice the difference
between what we are and what we do.

Very much alive.
Thinking in accidental future tense
while my kids skulk around trying
to scare me out of myself.
Saying *hoc est corpus meum.*
In a crisis I can't remember
if I'm supposed to survive or thrive

what's the difference
I hate competition.
This is a calendar; this is a death eater.
This the purple monk's hood that blooms
through fall, too poisonous to disappear
overnight. My problem
is feeling like it's linear

when I know it's not.
There are only so many ways to stop
a war, like a sacrifice, like time travel.
Declaring a winner in the sepia hour again.
But in the middle ground we see each other
both of us squinting into the distance
beyond the you.

Dear Wallace,

Did you love trouble? Somehow,
I doubt it. You craved
silence like the rest of us
but you were serious
in your quest
to hear the entire cacophony

seriously though
how did you feel about kids

I've always preferred the lowlier oaks
to the lofty pines (all-seeing
as they may be)

those branches bowed over in sympathy
like a lyric
or a search party.

*

And then there are those
who say everything's okay

on the one hand they have invention
and on the other the mothers
& between, an animal mind for a scale.

What was your father like?

Going back
does he remember
your body
        new
like she does?

Does he talk around
the teeth, evading
sacrifice?

Does your mother treat him
like an invention?

I think by now you know
I'm asking how we got here.

*

When Claudia read in this city
we loved her
because she brought the work
and everyone could see it.

There is a kind of building that happens
where condos go up
suddenly nothing can be obvious anymore
the views of the train track
blocked by a living wall
a lifestyle choice
or one made on our behalf.

The developers really are different from us
and not just because we see ourselves in the ruin
money is so romantic
we all get that
but we know what even one life means.

My first apartment
was full of blue and incense
and my friends came over
and got so high it hurt
when I got up at five to go to work and saw
all the futures against each other.

Have we become obnoxious?
Writing updates for the impatient
while the worthy spend their time
at the ocean or something.
Has nothing changed?

It's smoky in here, the bakery
burning things for the economy
enough and not at all
what we want.

We can't let it get past us, Wallace,
the urge to collect
the urge to destroy
the urge of every one of us
trying to get somewhere right now.

*

It's not so much
    the dates on the calendar
as the way we fill them
    it's not homage
but adage
    all the dead and buried brains
asking if anything happens
    next.

Dear Wallace,

Now we live in your rubble.
Capital waves its flags
first in gold, then white.
Each soldier gets a medal
made of earth turned over.

Am I lucky to do anything at all?
Let's make a soundtrack of failures,
play it over and over
while we play house.

Is my erasure your mother?

I think of the seasons I do live in
April's heave and July's burn
the way lilies exist at all.

We raise the dead
which is something.
I think I like it like that
even if I hate it here.

*

I don't know if I'll ever have that
je ne sais quoi
that defies the world
I may be too often pulling
the snail from its shell to see
its binding, whirling my eyes against
the window for a design
and our dinner. I'm a helper
in the way I might know what you mean.
Which is about as dumb as the wind.
Not what you mean, of course
but how I fuck it up.
Silence is golden, but a poem is now.
Is that why we call it
fool. Pull away from the glass.
The words we seek just
worker's comp for a case of charm.

*

In the end, I chose
a little better, a little worse
than you did, but we both end up
at the estate sale

a friend of mine keeps publishing everything
making money and I despise
her a little
what am I even moving toward

I too could have had quiet
but chose against those rooms
or did I

sometimes we call this the forgotten place
speaking past but thinking forward
to what I want to forget
or it just feels good to be a jerk
to some idea that stiffed me

who can I blame
when I followed a dream
so deep
it wasn't even mine anymore

this dumb forest already not
a forest
just a few creatures left
without a system

who can I be
like you
I'm nothing
but my ecology.

*

Pop! Oh, but the weasel
refuses. I have uttered
myself alive 'til it's done.
My paint applied in layers,
then chipped with same care.
My story full of—you guessed it—
words, like amaryllis, garish, mourning
her right season. Love! I turn
up the volume. Nonsense.
Meddling the canvas. Somewhere
in a basket of your remainders
the old world carries on.
Leave it: You'll have me now,
or nothing.

Dear Wallace,

Did you ever get a headache from darkness? Not migraine, mine; my groan or growth pain, some cave girl's misrest. Did you wonder about the women around you, their moods? I am sure they noticed yours, just tried to let it go. How often did you cry. I want to believe at least weekly, please. Enough to keep it flowing. A little leak in the cellar, some crack to see in the blind.

*

I'm sporting this autumnal reverberation
like I can't even *be* here without you,
right. Turning everything we touch
to more worthy than before.

A word, a place, a face, all caked with dying
color. I leave the doctor with a weird feeling
about my questions.

The air practices weather
and Americans begin to talk
about death. We indulge them.
A broken record of our living.

My mom introduced me to Joni Mitchell
when I was sixteen, after listening to Joni
when she was young
and then not listening to her
for sixteen years.

A little voice in my house,
seeing pictures just taken,
saying, *Those are some of my best memories.*

*

My kids don't cry at funerals
but cry to think the sun
will one day die too.

No one cries when winter leaves us.
But when it settles in, snow and all,
we cry for what we inherit.

If I leave anything
let it be a grimace followed close
by a cackle across the room.

All that I keep at an arm's length
is you. Up to the light
that left the sun
for me.

*

Lately the din
inhibits my thinking
so I lay low
to stay sharp

lately it's 4 degrees or 21 degrees or 39
and surfaces do not give
so I do
I give it all up
to the futures I've coded

lately the revolt is being realized
in the streets, as they say
but those must be other streets
yours are eerily quiet

though the noise is all about you
unlikely hero of a town
apparently you buried your heart in its sleeve
apparently heroes are personal
like monsters
one staying holy in the grave
the other unearthed for all to see.

Dear Wallace,

You were only here because
at some point someone made space for you

I too want a predictable home
so I can do whatever I want
but for you and for me this
translates differently

what people don't realize is
form is personal
for women form it's a kind of ending you know
we birth ourselves over and over
after each little death
an army of me

maybe we're only reinventing
capital like
music and flowers

to know work by another name

to know the names of love

to love the un-
doing
I mean we can't even agree
if resources are fixed or infinite

let me tell you
a resource is just a pocket
a rupture in the pattern
when the mothers part the waters
and everyone runs through.

NOTES AND ACKNOWLEDGMENTS

Some of the poems in this book (listed here by introductory line) first appeared in these journals:

Interim: [Why is your archive so dull?] and [Lately the din]

Phoebe Journal: [Fortunately, my kid was wrong]

Salamander: [They say mother is the boredom], [Many, many animals and insects], and [You were only here because]

the tiny: [The long tidal river], [You're prolific.], [If things change not for some time], [Your sentiment like a boulder], [So I've also wondered], and [Sanctuary.]

The Wallace Stevens Journal: [I guess you never had to listen], [Did you love trouble? Somehow,], [I wish you had written a], and [It's true that sometimes the sun]

Western Humanities Review: [We may share this same gray noon], [It's not so much], and [What if my urgency is the same]

The following lines (italicized in the poems) originate in these songs:

"It looks a lot like engine oil and tastes like being poor and small," from "Deep Red Bells" by Neko Case

"I want to be the one to walk in the sun," from "Girls Just Want to Have Fun" by Cyndi Lauper

"I do it for the joy it brings / because I'm a joyful girl," from "Joyful Girl"
by Ani DiFranco

"Lightning strikes maybe once / maybe twice" & "and the child was
enough," from "Gypsy" by Fleetwood Mac

"Some girls, some girls are only about / that thing," from "Doo Wop
(That Thing)" by Lauryn Hill

"Looking jealous or crazy," from "Hold Up" by Beyoncé

"Just to feel free and be someone" & "nobody gonna make me do things
their way," from "Born to Run" by Emmylou Harris

"Someday you will ache like I ache," from "Doll Parts" by Hole

"An army of me," from "Army of Me" by Björk

Some of the other italicized lines were borrowed from my own household,
with permission.

I am indebted to so many wonderful people who have supported the progress
of this book. To Lisa Moore, Aby Kaupang, B.K. Fischer, Marcela Sulak, and
especially Debora Kuan; the members of Brickwalk; Dennis Barone; Daniel
Coudriet; and the editors of all the journals that published early poems from
this collection: Thank you for truly seeing this work, for your careful read-
ing and your generous encouragement. To Hilda Raz and everyone at the
Backwaters and the University of Nebraska Press, my deepest gratitude for
selecting this manuscript and making a way for it. To the history of mothers
making art or searching for beauty in the labor of caring for others in a capi-
talist patriarchy, you have been my light. To Pallavi Dixit—what would I do
without you? To Jason, for your endless yes, and Cora, Omi, Leo, and the rest
of my family, thank you for being your whole selves, seeing the wildness of the
world with me, and making me laugh so very hard. I love you forever and ever.

INDEX OF FIRST LINES

My whole brain is here for it, 11

Today everyone managed 12

Sometimes I'm rabid as you. 13

Who carves the way for mothers? 14

Was it lovely 15

But this is a swamp, they said. 16

Many, many animals and insects 17

I wish you had written a 18

O what you managed! 19

Shall we go back and unname it? 20

Across the street 21

Though we inhabit the same place 22

It's true that sometimes the sun 23

Waiting in your neighborhood 24

An imposition: 25

Fortunately, my kid was wrong 26

Sanctuary. 27

The Backwaters Prize in Poetry was suspended from 2005 to 2011.

To order or obtain more information on these or other University of Nebraska Press titles, visit nebraskapress.unl.edu.

Printed in the USA
CPSIA information can be obtained
at www.ICGtesting.com
CBHW020937220824
13527CB00003B/81

9 781496 240064